Walking on the Boundaries of Change

Walking on the Boundaries of Change

Poems of Transition

by Sara Holbrook

Boyds Mills Press

This book is dedicated to Kelly and Katie, for helping me set the boundaries and then stretch them until they fit just right.

And special thanks to Dr. Amy McClure for her expert help in sorting and editing.

—S.H.

Walking on the Boundaries of Change

Day by day
a tightrope,
walking on the boundaries
of change.
One step —
firm, familiar,
the next step —
shaky, strange.

Some friends
will dare danger,
mock or push each step.
Some friends
knock your confidence.

Real friends
form a net.

A Different Fit

Sometimes
I feel so different —
a maple leaf
turned red in June,
displaying colors I can't quiet,
about as subtle
as a sonic boom.

Today
I want to fit in
another speck in the sparrow crowd.
Not be perched like ostrich in hiding
with embarrassing parts sticking out.

Why can't I gravel crunch along
with all the rest of the rocks,
instead of feeling like an alien
standing out
in neon socks?

Evolution

TV came
out of radio,
free verse
came out of rhyme.
I am
coming out of middle school
changing all the time.
It's time
to lose the water wings,
crawl out of this lagoon.
I want to stand upright.
Get on my feet.
I want it soon.

On the Rise

Everybody's changing,
it isn't like first grade,
valentines on the wall,
our hearts looked similar,
displayed.
We all stood to say the pledge,
we traveled in a line,
held two fingers up for quiet,
returned from recess,
every time.

Now we all have different destinations,
each our own speed,
each our own track.
Some seem lost
in the transition.
Can't go forward.
Can't go back.

They told us we were different,
little multi-colored snowflakes,
and we rose,
a swirl against brick buildings,
we rebelled.
Snowflakes.
No one told us.
Who would settle.
Who would fly.
And who
(and who?)
would melt.

Disappointment

Disappointment!
What a surprise —
You're a blast from door's-open-cold.
You're nuts in my chocolate cream.
You're a late lunch
    and bread sprouting mold.

Disappointment?
You're a blister from new favorite shoes.
You promised and then you forgot.
You're just crumbs where there
    once was a cake.
You looked honest, but then you were not.

Disappointment —
You took pliers and yanked out my trust
like a dentist without novocaine,
then you didn't return my calls
when I tried to express my pain.

Meant for Fun

It was just for fun —
a game of truth or dare.
No one meant to hurt.
No one meant to get so scared.

A game without a box,
a lid,
a single rule.
No one meant to dare real danger.
No one meant to be so cruel.

A game.
It was just for fun —
truth or dare,
we each could choose.
No one meant it.
Who could know —
that all of us would lose?

Finals

The accident.
The news.
Sped like a lighted fuse
to dynamite
our homeroom.

Facts were scattered
and confused.

Who was driving?
At what speed?
What road?
What curve?
What time?
How bad?
Oh, God.
Which tree?

Respirator. Coma.
Lifeflight. CPR.
Today's vocabulary words,
new adjectives
for "car."

The explosion left us staring,
unresponsive
with fixed eyes,
at
that blasted empty desk.
No retakes.
No good-byes.

Tough Enough?

Hey there,
tough guy,
arms,
a shield across your chest,
buttressing that wall.
I saw your anger flex
and I'm impressed.
You are a monument
to manhood.
I mean no disrespect.
But, pray,
brave knight,
could you
but step
out of your character
for just a little while?
I know
you're tough,
don't need a thing.
But I could use
a smile.

None of Your Business

"It's none of your business," means
keep your yap shut with dumb questions,
    I've made up my mind.
It means, *don't interfere*,
don't talk, I won't hear, and don't plead,
    'cause you make my teeth grind.

I've closed my brain doors.
It's a personal matter. I need time
    to noodle this out.
I can handle it fine. Put a sock in the chatter.
I'm too busy to tell you about
    what I'm thinking.

I'm thinking! I'm thinking! Stop breathing!
Stop blinking! Stop your,
    "I was just going to say."
And don't slap me around
with your sorry-faced frown. This time
    I'll do it my way.

Ducking Out

A drive-by.
It's a hit-and-run
by hurt.
You need to cry
to bleed your pain.
A little shower now,
just might avoid a
hurricane.
"Whoa!"
You're lightning fast with verbal fists,
your anger stabs and stabs the air.
"It wasn't me!"
I step aside to duck.
It doesn't mean that I don't care.

I can't answer for the hurt,
and I can't tell you what to do.
I can wrap your wounds with love,
but I won't bleed for you.

The Gun

I'm smarter,
stronger,
faster,
unless you have the gun.

I have pride
and self-esteem,
my stuff —
unless you have the gun.

You disrespect my freedom,
friends can't hold both guns
and hands.
You don't even have to shoot
before
you've ripped off who I am.

Un-named

Instinct
leads the cat to hunt,
although
he doesn't eat his prey.
His food comes in a bag,
he knows,
but he kills anyway.
Can domesticated animals
be entirely tamed?
Must cats
continue killing,
no matter what they're named?

Major Differences

Whenever
your kind sticks together,
my kind feels left out.
When your kind starts to whisper,
my kind starts to shout.

Your kind feels neglected,
my kind feels aggrieved.
We both feel disrespected,
both feel we've been deceived.

We divide the world in columns
when we stick to our own kind.
We nurture our suspicions,
keep our stereotypes in line.

We have to keep our distance
so we've another kind to blame.
How come,
if we're so different,
we both react the same?

A Choice

You can scold
or we can converse.
We can talk,
or we can curse.
Form a team
or fight to be first . . .
    but not both.

I can ask
or I can demand.
Shake my fist
or shake your hand.
We can walk together
or take a stand . . .
    but not both.

A state of mind,
a tone of voice.
Confrontation — cooperation,
a personal choice.
One or the other . . .
    but not both.

Being Tough

She won't say what she wants,
she's not the wanting kind.
She won't acknowledge need
or speak what's on her mind.

She says she can't feel hurt,
she won't play show and tell.
She talks of being tough.
Her eyes say something else.

A Real Case

Doubtful,
I have a fever
or any other measurable symptom.
I'm just down with a sniffly case
of sudden-self-loathing-syndrome.

TODAY!
It hit like a thwop of mashed potatoes
snapped against a plate,
An unrequested extra serving
of just-for-now-self-hate.

Today, I'm worthless,
a leftover bath,
a wad of second-hand gum.
I belong in a twist-tied bag
with the rest of the toys that won't run.

My mood's as welcome as
incoming dog breath,
or a terminal case of split ends.
I sparkle like a dust rag,
I could attract mosquitoes —
maybe — not friends.

In fact, I could be contagious!
I'm a downer to say the least.
And if you try to push
my mood swing, I'll only drag my feet.

Why? I couldn't tell you.
Just, some days, I get up and get down.
It's not a permanent disability, though.
Tomorrow,
I'll come around.

Two by Two

When I'd like to party, party, party,
you say, "I'd rather sit and veg."
When you'd like to shoot some hoops,
I yawn and truck on off to bed.

When you're up for holding hands,
I'm up for basketball.
When I'm so tired that I can't stand,
you say, "C'mon, let's take a walk."

Two by two
ain't easy.
Our clocks are set to different speeds,
neither one is wrong.
But we gotta synchronize
SOMETIMES
if we're going to get along.

Get It in Gear

If love is a go,
  trust is first gear.
Shift into threats,
  lying or fear . . .
you'll drop the transmission.
  Oops.
Love's out of commission.

A Secret Sonnet

I gently plucked a kiss from your left ear
and softly slipped it there, beneath your chin.
Sh . . . sh . . . we mustn't let the parents hear.
Shriek! They'll stomp and holler, "Mortal sin."
Let's not announce this so our friends will know.
Please, keep this interaction off the news.
They'll set alarms, keep asking, "Yes or no?"
Tick tock — the clock — and we will have to choose.

On one side, half will moan we went too far.
The rest will mock us, screaming out for more.
Reactions! You will spring to arm your guard
and I will shrink to barricade the door.
Entrenched in public we will sadly miss
the private chance to savor just one kiss.

Homecoming

Look here.
    I'm talking football.
And you?
    You're talking dance.
I hope we cream the Bears.
You're looking for romance.

I say we give it up.
We're like a mustard/jelly sandwich.
    Homecoming?
    You kidding?
You don't even speak my language.

Root Bound

Weeping willow,
    leafy fireworks,
        cascading to the ground.
Feathers in your hair,
    Rapunzel
        all let down.

"Look there," I said.
    That tree,
        her toes dipped in the stream.
A model for
    a fountain,
        dressed in shades of green.

"Those willow trees are filthy,"
    he said,
        they litter all around.
Their roots tie up the sewers,
    every one
        should be chopped down."

He is root bound by restrictions.
    You're a testament
        to free.
He can't peek beyond
    the boundaries of practical
        with me.

My Plan

As soon as I can
I'm going to buy a new nose.
Can you imagine THIS forever?
As soon as I can,
the beakface goes.
And then, who knows?
Could be I'll shorten my feet,
since they can't get out of the way.
Send my skin out for repair,
tune up this Minnie Mouse voice
and then I may
have a couple inches added here
and a couple more subtracted there,
have the points shaved off my elbows
and the slouch removed from my spine.
No more leaving the looks to chance,
I want a body by design.

My smile is too crooked to be loveable,
soon as I can, I want it straight.
Diets never work,
I'll suction off this extra weight.
Stop yapping about my future,
I have a long-range plan.
Right now?
I'm coloring my hair
and for good reason.
Because I can.

Amused

A muse.
The accidental thought,
the sticky ruse
my daydreams brought
that always makes me
tardier than bells.
Till someone yells
and hurry pushes
my dawdle to respond,
but not for long.
Until, again, I'm
interrupted by temptation,
another brief examination
of the mossy side of memory
kicked over in a haste,
I stop for just a taste,
the world will have to wait.
Again.
Again.
I'm late.

In Season

What is the summer for
but love —
its light
to fill
the empty room.
What is its way
but to be warm —
its destiny
to bloom?

Lost in Love

A balloon
one night,
no chart or plan.
I put my trust
in your open hand.
Below became
a spreading view
of who I was,
we rose into
the black,
above the flickering lights
of tentative love.
The speck that was me,
a fading face,
as off we drifted
into space.

Fast Love

Kissing Kristin's popular.
Real popular,
with boys.
A presidential candidate
would like
the fame that she enjoys.

It isn't 'cause
she's beautiful,
talented or smart.
She's just fast
and user friendly
like a quick-stop-dairy-mart.

Fast love
is like fast food.
Sometimes it looks
delicious.
But, it doesn't satisfy
because
it isn't that nutritious.

Kristin's not so bad,
she's on these food runs
all alone.
Trying to pick up
what's out-of-stock
at home.

Getting Told

My mama, she told me, "Be careful."
The boy, he told me he loved me.
My teacher said, "Don't be a fool, you stay in school."
The boy, he told me he loved me.
The TV says, "Practice safe sex."
The boy, he told me he loved me.
My dad said, I get pregnant, he's going to kick me out.
The boy, he told me he loved me.

Hear It?

I don't want to talk about *it*.
It's secret.
You wouldn't believe *it* anyway.
I'm locked.
I lost the key.
It doesn't matter what we say.
Nothing will change.
It's not that bad.
It doesn't bother me a bit.
It's my problem, anyway
and I can handle *it*.
It's a private hand I have to play.
It's about cards I cannot show.
It doesn't matter.
Go away.
It would be wrong for you to know.
I should have stopped *it* long ago.

I'm serious.
Leave me alone.
You can't understand *it*
or my fear.
Get out.
I have nothing to say.
Don't you get *it*?
Can't you hear?

Lies

I got burned, but
you can't say I was abused.
I'm just down
and feeling used.
My eyes are dark
but dry,
no one knows
about the lie.

I never should have smiled
and said
that everything's all right.
I should have said,
"Hold on,"
but I'm scared to spark a fight.

When I'm all buffed up
in smiles,
I can't say I'm victimized.
This arson is my crime.
I set fire to my insides
with a lie,
a smile
that let my hurting
hide.

Team Players

Teammates side by side,
cleat-crunch the cinder track,
spit projected at the grass
and slaps across the back.

When it's not yet graduation,
each loss can be undone
by a soda and a shower
and manliness is fun.

It's not like watching Dad
choked into a shirt and tie
jump-start himself with coffee
and briefly gruff, "Good-bye."

Playing like a man is part of
growing into one.
But where's the sport
when day after day
alarms you up like a starting gun?

Manhood's a lengthy season,
it's work to not get beat.
When everyday's a playoff,
must fun get obsolete?

Confidentially Speaking

We don't publicize
   our friendship
or all the fun we had.
I offer you a put-down,
   "Chump!"
And you return a jab,
   "Fool!"

We're not for talking sissy.
   We strike and spark
but don't explode.
It's highly confidential —
   a dot-dash-dot Morse code.

We poke.
We shove.
We jerk around
   and no one can suspect
that when we push away,
for a moment —
   we connect.

Investments

Securities
I've borrowed
from the pockets
of your mind,
and tucked them
secret places
to be returned
in kind.
A valuable investment
in friendship
has been made,
accumulating interest
in trust
for future trade.

Acting Spooky

This time not a headless horseman,
haunted castle
or vampire's coffin.
It's not midnight
or Halloween.
There's no face in the window
or ghoulish fiend
hiding underneath the bed.
This time the spooks
are in my head.

Am I crazy?
Naive?
Disrespected?
Confused?
They are talking about me.
I'm just being used—
Am I right?

Imagination can make me scared
when I see things that are not there.

Was I played for a fool?
Were they putting me down?
These ghosts in my head,
howling around—
Are they right?

I could jump out a window,
punch out or act out or
    STOP
to first check out
just what is real—
    Right?

Jealous

One on one,
Jealous
jump-reacts,
fouling out
when tossed a fact,
as sportsmanlike
as a leg-hold trap —
and just about as fun.

Saving for a Rainy Day

Does anyone ever forget
the ache of being ignored?
Can anyone ever forgive?
Or do hurts merely get stored
in a low interest,
savings plan way,
till some
dark, drippy
low-esteem day,
when festering
worthlessness fears
mature into insecure tears?

Run Away

I saw JoLynn just once
after she ran away.
We hugged at each other's eyes,
touched hands,
with little to say.

She said she was doing fine
until she lost her toothbrush.
She said she was better off.
I wondered what the truth was.

She traded
anger, control and unhappiness
at home.
She left
lugging a stubborn suitcase
she has to carry all alone.

When she was running into all those problems
she used to snap and spit like fire.
But, now that she's run away,
the heat is off —
she just looks tired.

Blown Away

There was never a rep like Tony's.
His was the coldest in the school.
In the library?
Check it out.
His picture's under "Cool."
He was exclusive,
an original,
we copied him
from his hair down to his stroll.
That was,
till Tony joined the Panthers
and the gang ate Tony whole.

Now, he wears their look,
their jacket,
their shoes,
their hat
and their tattoos.
He must have dumpster-tossed his brain.
He even wears their attitudes.

The Panthers
tell him where to go,
who to talk to,
what to say.
Tony better get a grip
before he's blown away.

For Real

This time
not a movie,
a song or a play.
This time
this kid
can't be scripted away.
He's here
performing his pusher act
I can't nice-nice
or not react.
This time
his sales pitch
in my face,
'til it's standing room only
in my personal space.
This time
my time
to say
good night,
turn my back
and exit right.

Just Say No?

Fine words on a billboard,
but can they take the heat,
where *just no* can leave me
in the fast lane or
alone down in the street.

Just no might sound more like a put-down
or attract too much attention.
Just no might even spark a fight or
could ignite somebody's tension.

Just no can sound like a whole speech,
or may be more than I want to say.
No one wants to hear me preach.
And so I just say,
not today.

Fast Chuck

No one said Chuckie
didn't have brains,
to him learning and talking
came fast.
Whether reading or rapping or math,
his ideas shot like fired rocket blasts.

He grabbed at new thoughts
like free candy,
never too much or enough.
He always had to be first,
even first learning all the wrong stuff.

Streetwise?
Now figuring angles
to get what his body
won't need, he is using
to keep himself going
on a desperate drive to succeed.

Fast Chuck.
Just racing to crash.
Skinny and jumpy with shakes,
his body is falling apart.
A rocket in a raggedy car,
a blast of fast,
but how far?

Until

It was nothing,
never mentioned
at dinners
and pass the tension.
Lips together
politely chewing,
not that tough,
a common stewing.

Never solved,
the problem
swallowed,
not resolved.
Each dinner balanced
by strength of will.
The family excused,
almost,
until . . .

Bang, I Gotcha

"I never needed you anyway, so there!"
    I shoot from the hip . . .
"I don't even care what you have to say."
    Words shot intended to rip
a bull's-eye wound near your
    nowhere heart.
"I'm better off on my own,
    apart."
I candle puff my smoking gun,
    holster my hurt.
Turn,
    and run.

Breaking Free

Freedom has no closets,
no inheritance to store.
It hides beneath no covers
in a room without a door.

Freedom jumps aboard tomorrow,
headed anyplace,
with no arrival times, no maps,
no traps nor travel case.

No appliances, like handcuffs,
burden Freedom's whim.
Freedom does without
so it can soar within.

Just Not Yet

Soon the ground
will be pushing up daisies,
a warming tray
for the summer lazies.
I window watch
for the gray to blush,
but days are days
and can't be rushed.
Those cherry blossoms,
dripping wet,
whisper delicious —
    just
        not
            yet.

Faces

Faces mirror
faces.
Looking through
our differences
can we comprehend
a community of learning
to read
past only faces
to human heart within?

Can the rhythm
of our language,
its twang
and brogue
and jive,
work to keep
the solo voice,
the chorus
and
the symphony
alive?

Leaving Messages

I talked to Mary-Virginia
I talked to Paulie.
I talked to the checkout guy at the store.
I talked to Beronica
about 100 times,
but I needed to talk some more.

So I talked to opposing teams
when we took a drink at halftime.
I called in on the radio
and talked to the aluminum siding help-line.

I talked to my journal.
I talked to the cat
and to my locker,
which
didn't help.
Nothing helped.
I couldn't get the message through
until
I bit my lip
and finally talked to you.

Recycling Center

Gloria's good at—other people's.
Other people's habits.
Other people's dress.
Other people's relationships.
Her stuff just sits there
and collects.
She sorts through other people's garbage
and ignores her rotting stash.
She's stinky,
and just keeps on recycling
other people's trash.

Rumors

Garbage in.
Garbage out.
The rumor input trail,
one story in the database
and the news is in the mail.

The facts
get gobbled byte by byte
as the fiction is repeated,
spreading like a virus.
The truth,
crowded from the memory,
is automatically deleted.

Creative Grades

Creative does,
'though not what's told,
a student
who is not enrolled
in graduated, chaptered classes,
where mindful competition passes
for excellence.

His recompense
is not achieved
by others brandishing respect.
Creative
grades its own neglect.

Honesty

Honesty
trying,
is more than
just simply
the absence
of
lying.

Midnight

When it's Sunday
and it's midnight,
the weekend
put back in its chest,
the toys of recreation,
party times
and needed rest.

When I lie in wait
for Monday
to grab me by the ear,
throw me at the shower,
off to school
and when I hear
the train at midnight
from so many miles away . . .
when it's Sunday . . .
and it's midnight . . .
the train
in passing brays and boasts
it's steel-track-straight,
on schedule,
arrival times to keep.
And I meander to its rhythm,
flopping like a fish.
Why can't I get to sleep?
Why can't I get to sleep?

A Sonnet All My Own

Success is not a flowery bouquet
that's handed off; it smells like dirty socks.
It ripens in my shoes as I make tracks
while hurdling and vaulting mental blocks.
Those stinky, sweat-soaked socks are not like hats
that I might lose or borrow from a friend,
they're change-resistant stores of self-back-pats
that let me feed my own receiving end.

No BRAVO! that the crowd may chant or yell
or pricey, bottled fragrance I might buy
can match the homegrown, confidential smell
success creates—a self-made, all-time high.
"I did it!" When I blossom on my own,
it outlasts any compliment on loan.

On the Verge

Look inside this block of marble —
see the angle of a chin?
See? This part juts out —
and here?
It slopes back in?

I know it's just a block of marble —
but see the profile?
Use the light.
A shoulder, outstretched arm,
it's stepping forward.
Am I right?

Museum walls are lined
with graceful statues,
polished rocks, smoothed
of all their edges.
Works of art
that once were blocks
like this.
Look here, a foot,
a hand, a nose,
an outline on the verge,
struggling to be seen.
A profile
trying to emerge.

Text copyright © 1998 by Sara Holbrook
Cover photograph copyright © 1998 by The Reuben Group

Published by Wordsong
Boyds Mills Press, Inc.
A Highlights Company
815 Church Street
Honesdale, Pennsylvania 18431
Printed in the United States of America

Publisher Cataloging-in-Publication Data
Holbrook, Sara
    Walking on the boundaries of change : poems of transition /
by Sara Holbrook.—1st.ed.
[64]p. : cm.
Summary: A collection of poems about issues facing young
adults, from new experiences to making choices.
ISBN 1-56397-737-0
1. Conduct of life—Juvenile poetry. 2. Children's poetry,
American. [1. American poetry.] I. Title.
811.54—dc21   1998   CIP
Library of Congress Catalog Card Number 98-70382

First edition, 1998
Book designed by Tim Gillner
Cover concept and photography by The Reuben Group
The text of this book is set in 12-point Caslon 540 Roman.

10 9 8 7 6 5 4 3 2 1